SEED MONEY IN ACTION

SEED MONEY IN ACTION

WORKING THE LAW OF
TENFOLD RETURN

by

JON P. SPELLER, D.D.

Robert Speller & Sons, Publishers
New York, New York 10036

PREFACE

In 1960, John Hoshor's wonderful SEED MONEY: THE LAW OF TENFOLD RETURN AND HOW IT WORKS was first published.

In the intervening years thousands of people have been helped through John Hoshor's account of the Great, but amazingly simple, LAW OF SEED MONEY.

He and I both thought that more people could be helped if they could know the Biblical references to the working of the Principle of Seed Money.

We both also thought that more people could be helped if they could see typical illustrations of the working of the Law of Tenfold Return with emphasis on HOW to overcome difficulties the reader may have in practicing it.

Accordingly, on May 3rd, 1962, John Hoshor gave me the right to expand SEED MONEY and to re-use the title. Thus is the origin of SEED MONEY IN ACTION.

All of John Hoshor's original SEED MONEY is included, with only slight changes in wording and form where it would be considered helpful to the reader.

I would like to thank those who have given me freely of their inspiration, example and teaching and who have thus helped me in my spiritual unfoldment.

The Rev. Dr. Paul M. Brunet, a Master teacher, guide, and inspiration. The Rev. Dr. Henry M. Ellis, who has unlocked the secrets of the Scriptures in his BIBLE SCIENCE: "THE TRUTH AND THE WAY." Dr. Henry A. Carns, President of The College of Divine Metaphysics, who has added dimensions to the Study of Life and the Word. Mrs. Claire Waters, Teacher at the Unity Center of Practical Christianity in New York, a perfect teacher of Truth. The Rev. Dr. David N. Moore, Minister and Practitioner who daily demonstrates his inspiringly high Consciousness.

The Reverend Daniel A. Watkins, my grandfather, a Methodist Minister for more than fifty years. The Most Reverend Eduardo Martinez Dalmau, Roman Catholic Titular Bishop of Theuzi, whose knowledge and practice of the Gospels are unsurpassed. The Most Reverend K. C. Pillai, Indian Orthodox Bishop, who has brought the simple Truths of many Orientalisms in the Bible into meaningfulness. Rabbi Dr. Abraham M. Hershberg, Orthodox Jewish teacher and scholar, who freely shares his wisdom and knowledge.

Last, but not least, three Great Ministers in

New York, each of whom has given wonderful sermons which have helped me as they have helped countless others:

The Rev. Dr. Raymond C. Barker, Minister of the First Church of Religious Science, at Town Hall.

The Rev. Dr. Ervin Seale, Minister of the Church of the Truth, at Philharmonic Hall.

The Rev. Dr. Eric Butterworth, Minister of the Unity Center of Practical Christianity, at Carnegie Hall.

All of these have helped me, as SEED MONEY IN ACTION is intended to help others prove for themselves the words of Jesus in Matthew 7, Verses 7 and 8:

"Ask, and it shall be given you; seek, and ye shall find; knock, and it shall be opened unto you:

"For every one that seeketh findeth; and to him that knocketh it shall be opened."

Jon P. Speller, D.D.

Seed Money in Action

SEED MONEY IN ACTION

Within the last five years many thousands of people have read John Hoshor's wonderful book, SEED MONEY: THE LAW OF TEN-FOLD RETURN AND HOW IT WORKS. Thousands have grasped the scientific principle behind the Seed Money Formula and have successfully applied it in their daily lives to end their money troubles. Others have not yet been able to use The Law of Tenfold Return — for different reasons. This book is to help these to prosperity — through Seed Money in Action.

John Hoshor wrote: "Let us imagine that we have $50 in United States of America currency.

"We could put the money in a Savings Bank and it would return us approximately $2 a year. We could buy a Mortgage Certificate and get a return of $3 or even $4 a year. Or we might use the money to buy a share or, depending on the price, several shares of stock in some corporation, perhaps get dividends and, provided we bought at the right time and sold at the right time, make a profit on the transaction.

"Of course, we could also use the $50 for

food, rent, clothing, books, tools or for other needs or just for pleasure.

"That is why money is the medium of exchange. It can be used for many things.

"One of the things for which money can be used — which at this writing is not generally known — is as SEED MONEY. This means that we can so use money that we reap a **harvest of multiplied money.**"

Here we have one of the first blocks some people have in using the Seed Money Principle.

A retired man called me long-distance from California. He said that he has read SEED MONEY, followed the formula faithfully, but could not get his return. It seemed that his greatest joy in retirement was driving his car through the beautiful California countryside. One day the old car just gave out — it couldn't go another mile and was towed to an auto grave-yard.

For two months the man tried to use Seed Money to demonstrate enough money to buy a new car. He gave his Seed Money to his Church, believing he would get his tenfold return — nothing happened.

He seemed to understand the principle clearly and to have complete faith in its work-ing. He puzzled me for a while. Then he said, "I better hang up. The call costs too much **filthy money.**"

I said, "Why do you say that money is filthy?"

His reply gave me the answer to his failure to receive his tenfold return: "Isn't money the root of all evil?"

I told him: "The Bible doesn't say that 'money is the root of all evil.' It says 'the love of money is the root of all evil,'• and even that needs explanation. In Biblical days money as we know it today was very seldom used. Most exchanges were on the barter system. A carpenter would exchange a table for some bushels of grapes. A farmer would exchange grain for clothing, and so on. Money, in gold and silver, was only used for big transactions.

"Today money is a universal medium of exchange for all good. When we fix it firmly in our minds that when we love money today we aren't loving the money itself, but the good it represents, we can and should actually love money. The Bible also says that you 'cannot serve God and mammon.'•• 'Mammon represents hoarded money — that which is not placed into circulation. Money in circulation is God in Action. Money which is hoarded is useless, for money is only a medium of exchange.

"You have had a hatred of money because you thought that it was evil. For many centuries

• I Timothy 6:10
•• Luke 16:13

our ancestors' common sense has told them that 'Like attracts like.' Thus through your hatred of money you have been repelling it from your life.

"Don't think of money as a dead object of greed. Think of it as a living means of acquiring good for yourself and for everyone. For example, right now, it represents in your life a new car with which you will enjoy the beauties of God's countryside."

He thanked me and two weeks later I heard from him again. "It's marvelous," he said with great joy in his voice, "I received my tenfold return. Yesterday my married daughter drove up from Los Angeles in her Volkswagen. She gave me the keys, telling me that her husband had just bought her a new station wagon so that they and their children could go on camping trips in the mountains. She knew that my old car had given out, so instead of selling the Volkswagen, she gave it to me."

"Wonderful," I said.

"You know," he said, "once I realized that it wasn't money for money's sake that I wanted through Seed Money, but the good I could buy with it, I overcame the mental block which had prevented me from receiving my tenfold return. The Volkswagen is worth even more than ten times my Seed Money, and on top of that it doesn't use as much gas as my old car — I can travel much farther for the same money!"

This is just one illustration of how a man's changing of his concept of money enabled him to use the Seed Money Principle. Have you been thinking of money as evil? Or have you been thinking of money as the good it represents in your life?

John Hoshor wrote: "Just **how** do we plant SEED MONEY? What happens when we do plant it?

"We **give** it to our Church or to a hospital, school or college or to any of the Social Service organizations which subsist on donations. Or, if we so wished, we could give it to any needy person, friend or stranger.

"Then we follow a specific mental formula derived from the Great Teacher and proven absolutely true and dependable by such financial giants as the first John D. Rockefeller, Andrew Carnegie, Julius Rosenwald, Andrew Mellon and others of great wealth.

"**With perfect safety, without any risk whatever, our SEED MONEY so planted will return to us tenfold. We will receive back $500.**"

Here is the second block often found in people who have not yet succeeded in practicing the Principle of Seed Money.

Many people don't understand how the giving of Seed Money produces its tenfold return **without any risk whatever**. But it is a fact. The Law of Tenfold Return ALWAYS WORKS.

There is absolutely **no risk whatever** in the Principle of Seed Money. If you do not follow the formula precisely there is risk, but then you are not actually practicing the Principle.

I received a rather irate letter from an airplane stewardess flying on charter flights out of Chicago. She wrote: "Mr. Hoshor's Seed Money doesn't work. I know because I tried it. When I fly to Las Vegas I play the slot machines. Sometimes I win. With Seed Money I don't get back a dime."

Writing back to her I gently informed her that the Seed Money Principle itself ALWAYS works but that she apparently is not really practicing it.

As illustration I wrote that the Principle of the Parachute is itself infallible. A properly made, properly packed, properly checked, and properly used parachute never fails to open.

If the parachute is not made properly, is not packed properly, is not checked properly or is not used properly it will not open. That is not the fault of the Principle of the Parachute or of the parachute itself. It is the fault of the person or persons who made, packed, checked or used the parachute.

The Principle of Seed Money works in the same way as the Principle of the Parachute, or as any other Principle, for that matter. If the

Principle isn't properly applied you aren't working the Principle.

The Seed Money Principle is not a gamble, such as a slot machine or a lottery. When you think that you **may** get your tenfold return from your Seed Money — you **won't**. When you believe that you **will** get your tenfold return from your Seed Money — you **will**.

Jesus said, "What things soever ye desire, when ye pray, **believe** that ye receive them, and ye shall have them."* He did not say that you **won't** have them. He did not say that you **might** have them. He said that you **shall** have them.

The "magic" word Jesus used there is "believe". There is no room for chance in believing. There is no room for chance in the Law of Tenfold Return.

I advised the stewardess to only practice Seed Money when she felt that she could remove all doubts about receiving her return. If she couldn't try to remove her doubts I advised her to forget it.

Two months later I received another letter from the stewardess. She said that her reason for desiring her tenfold return was because she wished to have enough money to visit her fiancé in the U.S. Air Force at Wiesbaden,

* Mark 11:24

Germany. As a non-scheduled domestic airline stewardess she didn't have the advantage of the reduced fares which most airline employees have. She said that with one week's meditation on the Principle of Seed Money — after she had received my letter — she had become convinced that the Law of Tenfold Return worked in Principle and that she could apply it to attain her desired trip. She gave ten dollars, following the formula properly in every step, to her Church that Sunday. On the following Wednesday she received an offer to take the place of a MATS (Military Air Transportation Service) stewardess on a European flight—to Wiesbaden Germany.

Her tenfold return? She called her parents to tell them of her new assignment. Her father told her that he had just received the return of his income tax overpayments. He sent her a gift of one hundred dollars for extra spending money.

This is just one illustration of many describing people who give, and give, and give Seed Money — without really believing that they will ever get their return. They don't, until they really believe that they will.

Do you think that you only **may** get your tenfold return? Or do you **believe** that you **will** get your tenfold return?

Some people have the same problem the

stewardess had, but in a different way. They give their Seed Money to their Church, believing that they will receive their return. Then a member of their family, a friend, a co-worker or some other person scoffs at their belief. Doubt seeps in. Their return is deflected. The Law of Tenfold Return doesn't seem to work for them.

John Hoshor writes: "Can't you just see the bankers and the economists holding up their hands in horror at Seed Money? They will tell you it cannot be done.

"You are welcome to believe them and lay this booklet aside or give it to someone else. Or you can read it and learn how SEED MONEY multiplies, why it multiplies and by following the principles and methods set forth prove its truth for yourself.

"Incidentally, it has often been said, many times inaptly, that 'The truth shall make you free.' The only truth that will make you free is the truth which you prove for yourself. If you cannot prove it in your own experience — if you cannot apply it and demonstrate it in your daily life — whatever it is, truth or not, it will not make you free."

A housewife visited me with the complaint that her husband didn't believe that the Seed Money Principle really worked. "He laughs and calls it a fool's gimmick," she said, "he keeps me from receiving my tenfold return."

I told her that "No one can prevent you from receiving your tenfold return except for you yourself. Your husband's remarks cannot prevent your tenfold return unless you yourself give them the power to do so."

As Ernest Holmes wrote in his great book, THE SCIENCE OF MIND, "**Nothing can happen to us unless it happens through us.** That which we refuse to accept, **to us cannot be, and** that which to us **is**, cannot help becoming a reality in our lives."

I asked her to remove the blocks caused by her acceptance of her husband's remarks by denying that they had any effect on her exercise of the infallible Principle of Seed Money. I asked her to affirm that she, and she alone, puts the Power and Abundance of the Universe into motion for her tenfold return.

I asked her, recognizing her great faith in the promises of the Scriptures, to recite — as an addition to the Seed Money Formula — when giving her Seed Money: " 'Surely blessing I will bless thee, and multiplying I will multiply thee.'° So God has promised. So is it with my tenfold return."

Six weeks later the housewife paid me another visit. She was now practicing the Law of Tenfold Return successfully. There was an interesting sequel. Her husband, seeing his

° Hebrews 6:14

wife's success with Seed Money — despite his scoffing — secretly started applying the Seed Money Principle himself. He finally, rather sheepishly, told his wife, "It works." And it does work.

The Law of Tenfold Return does not only work here and now, but forevermore in the future. The Law of Tenfold Return has ALWAYS worked throughout the Ages.

John Hoshor writes: "Long ago the prophet Malachi knew about SEED MONEY. A prophet becomes a prophet because he is inspired to rise to higher levels than most people and thus can more clearly see things and know things for what they really are."

Malachi said: "Bring ye all the tithes into the storehouse, that there may be meat in mine house, and prove me now herewith, saith the LORD of hosts, if I will not open you the windows of heaven, and pour you out a blessing, that there shall not be room enough to receive it."[*]

In present day words Malachi's inspired statement means that you should give your Seed Money to your Church, so that as you freely give so you shall freely receive, and it will be proved NOW, declares the Law of Tenfold Return, that the horn of Infinite Plenty shall be opened and pour you such an Over-

[*] Malachi 3:10

flowing Abundance of Good that you shall not have room enough to consume it.

A man I know is in the printing business. He was one of the printers of John Hoshor's SEED MONEY. His business had taken a turn for the worse. His printing presses were idle more often than they were busy. His overhead— rent, payroll, mortgage, etc. — was pushing him deeper and deeper into debt.

He asked me, "Does Seed Money really work?"

I told him, "Of course — when you follow the formula faithfully, the Law of Tenfold Return always works. It is simple **CAUSE and EFFECT.**"

"But can I receive as much as I need?" he said.

"Nothing can limit what you receive except for your own consciousness," I replied, "do you know the Twenty-Third Psalm?"

"Yes," he said.

I counseled, "Then remember David's words: 'Thou preparest a table before me in the presence of mine enemies: thou anointest my head with oil; **my cup runneth over.'*** It doesn't say **could** runneth; it says **runneth.** Isn't that definite? It doesn't say half full. It doesn't say full. It says runneth **over.** Isn't more than enough, enough?"

* Psalms 23:5

"Yes," the printer said. I could see that he understood. Several months later I called him to order another five thousand copies of Seed Money.

He said, "My business is running at more than capacity. Even with overtime I can't keep up with the demand. Thanks to Seed Money. But I'll print the books for you and Seed Money the overtime charges."

This printer is now so prosperous that he spends three months of every year in Florida. Thanks to his understanding and practicing of the Principle of Seed Money.

Do you demonstrate ten times a dollar, but fail at ten times ten dollars or ten times one hundred dollars? Or do you know that the Law of Tenfold Return works equally well on a thousand dollars as it does on a single dollar?

The only limitation of your return is caused by yourself. As Dr. Raymond Charles Barker of the First Church of Religious Science in New York City says: "All causation is from your subconscious mind, and your subconscious mind can be changed. You are the only one who can change it."

You alone can affect your reaping of your tenfold harvest — regardless of the amount involved.

As John Hoshor says, "Were Malachi around today to witness for us he would tell you that our $50 planted as SEED MONEY and properly cultivated would certainly return us $500 and that other SEED MONEY sums would return proportional harvests."

As money is solely a medium of exchange, your tenfold return is not necessarily in the form of currency. John Hoshor cited how a friend of his proved Malachi's promise with typewriters:

"My friend Sigmund was studying to be a writer. He felt that he could progress faster if he had a typewriter. Sigmund asked me to help him demonstrate a typewriter. I agreed and we started to work that night.

"Although Sigmund had often been writing at his desk when his landlady came to straighten up the apartment, the very next morning she suggested that he go to the basement and get the typewriter some folks who had once lived there had left. She told Sigmund that he might have the typewriter.

"Sigmund phoned that day and gave me an account of what had happened. He said, however, that the machine was not new and that he had taken it to have it cleaned and put in working order.

"The following day Sigmund picked up the typewriter and asked me to come and see it. I went to his place. I'm quite certain that it was not the first typewriter ever manufactured, but it could have been the second. The two of us sat quietly and looked at it.

" 'Does it work?' I asked him.

"Sigmund laughed and said, 'It does, in a manner of speaking.'

"During the next few weeks the machine needed fixing several times and Sigmund told me that he had finally decided to leave it in the repair shop.

"Soon after I was called to Phoenix, Arizona where I spent several months. When I returned to California I went again to see Sigmund.

"He asked, 'Why don't we try the type-writer demonstration again?'

" 'Let's apply what we learned from the other effort,' I suggested.

" 'We know that typewriter period is not enough,' Sigmund said.

" 'What kind of machine do you want?"

"Sigmund thought and answered, 'It doesn't have to be new but it should be a late model of a standard make and also be in good working condition.'

"I said, 'All right, that's our pattern, a late model standard make in perfect working order.'

"We both went to work on it that night.

"It was three days before I spoke with Sigmund again. He phoned and said that he had tried to reach me the day before. I explained that I had been away on a business appointment and asked what had happened.

"Sigmund said, 'A friend of mine who's been drafted into the Army brought me a typewriter that is only three months old. I once lent him my car to drive his mother to Seattle and he said he didn't know when he'd need the type-writer again, if ever, and he wanted me to have it.'

"I asked, 'What kind of condition is it in?'

" 'Perfect,' was Sigmund's answer.

"I said, 'Fine.'

"Sigmund said, 'That's not all. You remember my telling you about my friends who live across the street?'

" 'The ones for whom you mowed the lawn when the man had his ankle broken?' I asked.

" 'The same. When I came back from the store this afternoon, Mary — she's the wife — called me over. They are going back East and have more than they can haul in their car. They bought a typewriter a couple of years ago when they tried out the mail order business at home, but the business didn't prosper so they gave me the machine. Mary said that they had been watching me writing in longhand at my window and they wanted me to have it. I couldn't refuse it so I brought it home with me.'

"I said, 'Great. Is it in good condition too?'

"Sigmund said that it was in perfect condition. Then I pointed out to him that we had demonstrated two typewriters. I heard him laughing over the phone.

"I asked, 'What are you laughing about?'

"He answered, 'I have three. This morning when I went for the mail there was an almost new machine in front of my apartment door with a typewritten note — This is a gift — I thought that perhaps you had sent it.'

"I told him, and I told him truthfully, 'Sigmund, not only did I not send it, I know nothing at all about it.'

"Sigmund said, 'We'd better turn it off. I don't want to go into the typewriter business.'

"Since those years Sigmund has used the formula time and again and is today a prosperous writer and lecturer on the subject."

The demonstration of Sigmund's typewriters is an illustration of but one of many articles of value received in accordance with the Law of Tenfold Return. When my wife was approaching the time of the birth of our first child, we moved from Manhattan to an apartment in Kew Gardens. Our child was still to be delivered in the hospital in Manhattan where we had already made arrangements.

It was a wintry January in New York, and we didn't have a car. We applied the Law of Tenfold Return to demonstrate transportation for the day when our baby would arrive.

Although on the day when my wife had to go to the hospital the weather was so bad that most people could not find a taxi — we had not one, not two, but three vehicles to take us to the hospital.

Leo and Olga, a couple we know, were there with their car. Another friend, Pete, dropped by with his car. And a taxi I had called also arrived.

I gave the taxi to some people who couldn't locate a cab. The taxi-driver was surprised when I put a dollar in his hand anyway. He didn't know that it was Seed Money.

Olga and Leo drove us to the hospital in Manhattan. Pete asked if he could drive my wife and the baby back to Queens on the day when they would be released from the hospital. Little did he know that the ten dollars in taxi fares which he would save us represented tenfold return of the dollar I had given to the driver of the taxicab.

The day came when my wife and new baby daughter were released from the hospital. It was also the day after a big snow-storm. Pete's car was snowed under — we had no shovel to dig out the wheels.

I started an Affirmation. I had hardly finished when seemingly from nowhere a very small boy carrying a very large shovel appeared. He had been shoveling sidewalks and had noticed our plight. In no time the car was free from the snow and ice and we were on our way to Manhattan.

The Law of Tenfold Return can fulfill every desire. It is not limited by price. It is not limited by lack. As John Hoshor wrote:

"The resources of the Infinite are Infinite, and every human being has direct access to these resources.

"Jesus knew about SEED MONEY and how to multiply it. He referred to it more than a few times and with the loaves and fishes demonstrated it with great success before a huge throng.

"In the parable of the talents Jesus told about three men. One had been given one talent, another had been given two talents and the third had been given five talents.

"A Roman talent was a denomination of money approximately equivalent to $500.

"The man who had the two talents doubled his, as did the man who had the five talents. They were each commended and promised: "thou hast been faithful over a few things, I will make thee ruler over many things."* In effect this was saying that the principle they had applied could be used over and over again ad infinitum, that it was Unlimited in its operation.

* Matthew 25:21 & 23

"The man who had one talent did not multiply it but instead buried it in the ground. He was reprimanded and told that his one talent would be taken from him.

"Use part of your money as SEED MONEY and you will become prosperous, exceedingly prosperous."

In the parable of the talents Jesus illustrated why many people fail even today in their attempts to practice the Principle of Seed Money.

The man with the one talent — who failed to increase it — explained: "I was afraid, and went and hid thy talent in the earth."°

Many people who sometimes attempt to work the Law of Tenfold Return fail through **fear** — created and perpetuated only by themselves. The Law of Tenfold Return is only the orderly working of God in our minds, our bodies, and our affairs. On United States dollar bills is written "IN GOD WE TRUST" — very good advice.

Those who do not receive their tenfold return because of fear that it is lost, lose their money as surely as the man who buried his talent in the ground ultimately lost his. In trusting God one cannot fear — and the Principle of Seed Money demands absolute trust in God— Omniscience, Omnipotence, Omnipresence.

° Matthew 25:25

A doctor wrote to me that he could see the scientific basis of the Principle of Seed Money in harmony with the fundamental One Law of the Universe — but he couldn't overcome the gnawing fear that his Seed Money would be lost.

I wrote him what Job had said: "For the thing which I greatly feared is come upon me, and that which I was afraid of is come unto me."*

I told him that the Law of Tenfold Return knows no evil. If one fears that he will lose what he has, he will surely lose what he has, for his thoughts of fear express what he wants.

The doctor realized the boomerang caused by his fear — one that had cost him not only his tenfold return, but had caused him a tenfold loss. He saw the truth in Jesus' words: "For unto every one that hath shall be given, and he shall have abundance: but from him that hath not shall be taken away even that which he hath."**

Today the doctor has banished the word "fear" from his vocabulary. Through the Principle of Seed Money he has built up a flourishing and satisfying practice. He gives a copy of SEED MONEY to every new patient.

John Hoshor put it: "Fail to use money

* Job 3:25
** Matthew 25:29

as SEED MONEY and you will remain or become needy. Why? Because the needs of Life are forever eating up your Substance, your earnings, your capital. These must be constantly replenished and extended — renewed — just as you have to forever renew your Breath of Life.

"A very small percentage of our population today uses the Law of Seed Money in one form or another. These are the rich, and especially, the very rich. Yet, perhaps one in ten thousand of these few uses the Seed Money Principle consciously, knowing what they are doing. The others have conditioned themselves to follow certain business practices, some of which are not contrary to the Law of Seed Money and which, part of the time at least, are harmonious with that Law. Their financial success is in direct proportion to how closely they follow that Law.

"It should go without saying that success will be greater where one practices the Seed Money principle consciously and constantly than where one uses it only spasmodically and accidentally."

"A typical business operation in harmony with The Law of SEED MONEY might be as follows: A man gets an idea for a new product which will confer benefit upon those who buy it. He takes the idea to a friend. They study it and agree that people will buy it and be pleased with having and using it. They also agree it will require X dollars to develop and market the product. They calculate that they can sell the item in volume and estimate that they can profit to the extent of ten times the X dollars they must invest in it. So they go into business, follow their agreed course and make the profit.

"Details will differ in every case but the foregoing operational procedure is that utilized in almost every successful business venture."

A man telephoned from the South. He said that he was down to his last two hundred dollars. The only other thing he owned was some worthless land on the outskirts of his town. He had no prospects of any income.

I told him that "the earth is full of the goodness of the Lord."* This doesn't mean that the earth is empty of good, nor only half full of good. It means that the earth is full of good.

When you have a full dozen eggs you don't have six, you don't have eleven — you have twelve, the full dozen. Our good is exactly the same. With God there is no short-changing.

But your supply is only equal to your demand, and it is up to you to make your own demand on the Infinite. There is no lack of supply, only a lack of demand. You have to claim what you want, not what you don't want.

* Psalms 33:5

When you plant your Seed Money and claim "weeds" — you can't expect to receive a harvest of abundance of anything but "weeds".

A little tree in Canada serves as a fine example.

The Jack Pine was once a "weed." It was not only too small to use for lumber, but a substance within its cellular structure prevented its use for pulp in the manufacture of paper. Jack Pine was considered a "tree weed," with little present value and none foreseeable.

Millions of acres of Jack Pine were considered waste land — an area larger than the State of Connecticut.

But men of a paper company in Michigan **believed** "that a weed is merely a plant for which man has not yet found a use." They did what others considered impossible. They found an economical way to remove the substance contained in Jack Pine's cellular structure which had prevented its use for paper pulp.

As a result, this firm is now making a beautiful, high-quality paper out of Jack Pine — employing many thousands in this work.

Those who claimed nothing from Jack Pine — received nothing. Those who planted their seeds, **believing** in their own success — reaped the harvest.

I told the Southerner that he must not try to select a specific channel for the transmission of his return to him, that correct use of the Seed Money formula leaves the means of providing the tenfold return to its ultimate source, God.

As Eric Butterworth of the Unity Center in New York affirms in his book, UNITY: A QUEST FOR TRUTH:

"GOD IS MY ALL - SUFFICIENT RESOURCE. HE IS MY INSTANT, CONSTANT, AND ABUNDANT SUPPLY."

Dr. Butterworth further explains:

"God is my supply, everywhere evenly present, and as immediately available as the air I breathe. The moment a need arises in my life, God's infinite substance is immediately at hand to fill it. I am a child of God, and it is right and good that I manifest abundance. As God's child, I have been given the wisdom and intelligence to bring into expression all that is needed for my well-being and comfort. God inspires me with good judgment in handling the supply that is already mine, and opens the way to greater good, greater blessings, greater opportunities."

I asked the Southerner to reflect on this when he wondered about the source of his tenfold return. He promised to do so.

Nearly a month later I heard from him again. The Sunday after I had talked with him he had given a check for his entire two hundred dollars to his Church, absolutely sure of his tenfold return.

The next day he was visited by a newcomer to town. The newcomer told him that the town needed a driving range for its many avid golfers. He told the Southerner that his "worthless" land on the outskirts of town was ideal for that purpose. He offered to lease the property, put up the capital to make the driving range, and pay him a percentage of the gross receipts.

The Southerner received a down payment of two thousand dollars—ten times his gift to his church—and subsequently will make a comfortable living from his share of the proceeds from the driving range.

His prosperity is only a very small sample of what can be received through practicing the Principle of Seed Money. The Law of Tenfold Return can make you, as it says in the line from the song, **Pennies from Heaven,** "as rich as Rockefeller." John Hoshor wrote:

"The greatest fortune the world has ever seen in private hands was amassed by a man who thoroughly knew, understood and **constantly used** the Law of Seed Money.

"The first John D. Rockefeller, throughout his long life, put his full trust in that Law.

"Whether in his early days when he gave frugally, but regularly, to his Church or in his middle and later years when his foundations were giving many millions to better the world

Rockefeller always envisioned the many times multiplication of his gifts returning to him.

"And they did. How they did.

"Rockefeller knew the truth of the early Biblical promise, 'all the land thou seest shall be yours'. He laid his claim on the Infinite and accepted possession. It came to him. The Law always works.

"Rockefeller kept his secret a secret. He taught only his family, and the principle of Seed Money is still working full time for them.

"The world regarded the elder Rockefeller's practice of giving a new dime to everyone he met as a rich man's idiosyncrasy, but to Rockefeller it was a deeply religious and significant act, each gift another opportunity to multiply his return. Selfish? Greedy? Do not believe it. Here was a man in love with the Law, thoroughly and all-absorbingly in love with the law. He embraced the Law and it gave, flooded Abundance and Wealth and Prosperity over him almost beyond human power to count.

"Van Loon in his Life of Rembrandt paints a scene where the bailiffs are moving out the artist's stove and other furniture. In one corner of the hut his wife is lying on a pallet of straw dying of consumption. And what is Rembrandt doing? Standing in another corner of the hut painting. As Rembrandt was in love with paint-

ing, the first John D. was in love with making
the Law of Seed Money work for him.

"Many men have walked our earth and left
it richer for having been there, but it might
well be that this first John D. Rockefeller, once
probably the most reviled man of his era, left
behind for the human race riches as great as any
man who has been on earth.

"Rockefeller knew the Law and knew it so
well that when in his middle 40's America's
finest physicians gave him but six months to
live he took the Law and started applying it to
his health. As a result he outlived all of those
good medics from 25 to more than 40 years."

History has recorded John D. Rockefeller's
practice of Seed Money, which he started at the
earliest age. Before he had reached twenty-one
he was giving $1.80 per month to his church—
out of a salary of only $3.50 per week.

John D. Rockefeller, Jr. gave us proof of his
father's adherence to the Law: "I have been
brought up to believe, and the conviction only
grows upon me, that giving ought to be entered
into in just the same careful way as investing."

He also revealed that his family did not
accumulate its vast wealth for purely money's
sake—a negation of the Law—for "Money itself
is lifeless, impotent, sterile . . . but man with
his brain, brawn and imagination, using money
as servant, may feed the hungry, cure the dis-

eased, make the desert places bloom, and bring beauty into life."

That the Rockefellers knew that the Seed Money Principle is a Divine Immutable Law is revealed in John D. Rockefeller, Jr.'s creed:

"I believe in an all-wise and all-loving God, named by whatever name, and that the individual's highest fulfillment, greatest happiness, and widest usefulness are to be found in living in harmony with His will."

John Hoshor cites other notable large-scale beneficiaries of the Law of Tenfold Return:

"Andrew Carnegie, Julius Rosenwald and Andrew Mellon all knew the Law of Seed Money and practiced it throughout long and extremely prosperous lives. Not only did the gifts of these men enrich the entire world, but they also multiplied their personal wealth, because each of them knew how to claim the multiplied return of his gifts and constantly did so claim."

It was Andrew Carnegie who revealed that the truly great fortunes were not received through the worship of money for money's sake. He said that there is "no idol more debasing than the worship of money." Andrew Carnegie gave and received in his lifetime more than $350,000,000.

It was Julius Rosenwald who revealed that the truly great fortunes were not received through hoarding, but through circulating money —giving and receiving freely. He said: "I believe that under no circumstances should funds be held in perpetuity." Julius Rosenwald gave and received in his lifetime more than $60,000,000.

Andrew Mellon, although he was a public figure—he served for a time as U. S. Secretary of the Treasury—was one of the most secretive of the great practitioners of the Principle of Seed Money. He knew that no thoughts of others could possibly get into his mind to interrupt his application of the Law if no one knew of his system of multiplying his wealth. Thus Andrew Mellon burned the notes of small debtors at Christmastime and gave away his money in large bundles with the greatest of secrecy. It is said that he gave and received in his lifetime in excess of one billion dollars.

Some of the money these very wealthy practitioners of the Principle of Seed Money gave was in the form of the Biblical tithe. But the bulk of the money given was not ten per cent of what had long been received—but ten per cent of what was actually received in the consciousness of these men. That was how the money multiplied, through these men's perfect understanding that "whatsoever a man soweth, that shall he also reap".*

* Galations 6:7

Six hundred years before Jesus' Great Ministry, the Buddha in India also taught among his Sayings: "As we sow, so shall we reap." The Law, unlike the tithe, is not restricted in its Universality.

John Hoshor says of the tithe, "Practically everyone knows about the tithe. The tithe meant that one-tenth of the person's income belonged to the Church. It was, in effect, a payment due— a thanks-giving. More than a few are reported to have used the tithe and to have become highly prosperous doing so.

"There is a distinct difference between the tithe and Seed Money. The tithe is a gift AFTER you have made the income. Seed Money is a gift in order to claim a TENFOLD RETURN. Seed Money applies the Law directly, and therefore much more effectively. In utilizing the Seed Money Principle you are saying in effect: 'Here's the SEED I plant. Here's the investment I make with God. Here's the money with which I bless my fellow beings. I claim my tenfold return. I am drawing on my Unlimited account with the Infinite.'"

An elderly lady asked me, "Why do I have to run so hard to stay in the same place? I've given my tithe for forty years."

I told her that many people have become prosperous through use of the tithe—but generally through their conscious understanding of its direct effect on their financial well-being. I suggested that she continue her tithing, but add recognition that as she freely gives, so shall she freely receive. I gave her a copy of SEED MONEY.

The Seed Money Principle changed this lady's life. She grasped it with the greatest of ease. Now she circulates an ever-increasing amount of money in her life. She not only helps many people—but at the same time she now can afford many luxuries she had once denied herself.

Another man I know was up to his ears in debt. He never seemed to be able to catch up with his bills. I showed him these passages in SEED MONEY:

"Paying debts is one of the primary requisites of becoming prosperous. Some may think that they can achieve prosperity by never paying anyone. This is contrary to the Law and simply will not work. Something for nothing is always nothing. You must either pay as you go or pay later with interest compounded.

"The best practice for prosperity is to pay your debts before they are due, insofar as it is possible, and so keep them out of your consciousness."

The man said, "That's very true—but I'm in a

situation where that amounts to advice to close the barn door after the cow has been stolen. I sow my Seed Money, but the only return I've been getting is more harassment from my creditors."

I told him that apparently his resentments to his creditors and to himself were blocking his tenfold return. This resentment is the same as a boulder blocking a highway—if you don't remove the boulder once and for all it will roll back and impede your way again. The Prophet Jeremiah records this wonderful statement: "I will **forgive** their iniquity, and I will **remember** their sin **no more**."* You must forgive your creditors and forget your resentments toward them.

And it is also important that you forgive yourself—you cannot really forgive others without forgiving yourself. Nor can you really forgive yourself without forgiving others. The Lord's Prayer makes this very clear: "And **forgive us** our sins; for we **forgive every one** that is indebted to us."**

This man gradually understood the message. He has cast aside his resentments toward his creditors; he has ceased his self-condemnation. Now, through the Law of Tenfold Return, he is almost completely out of debt.

* Jeremiah 31:34
** Luke 11:4

This man, because of his great need, had asked: "Why can't I demonstrate more than ten times my Seed Money?"

I read to him from John Hoshor's SEED MONEY:

"Why tenfold and not elevenfold or twenty-fold or thirty-fivefold or a millionfold?

"Simply because the number 10 is the easiest of all to multiply by. You merely add a zero to the figure with which you start. The zero is symbolical, meaning that it is nothing to the Infinite to send you your multiplied return, that to the Infinite it is less than the air you breathe.

"Why not a millionfold?

"**Because you must be able to conceive yourself as having the amount you claim.**

"In fact, you MUST imagine that you **already** have it.

"Let us say we plant—give—$50 in accordance with the Law of Seed Money and lay our claim on the Infinite for $50,000,000 in return. Then we begin to wonder where all that money is coming from. We begin to doubt. The doubt shuts off our return, creates a block. It will be the doubt that we demonstrate.

"So the proper method is to start the process of giving—planting—but plant no more than you can conceive yourself as receiving in return ten-fold. Then lay positive claim to that."

This man understood the answer to his question from that. Others needed a more detailed explanation.

One such young man said: "The Law knows no limitation. If I can visualize one hundred or one thousand or one millionfold return on my Seed Money, why can't I do it?"

I answered, "If you can visualize such a return—and hold it unwaveringly—you can do it. Jesus said: 'If ye have faith, **and doubt not,** ye shall not only do this which is done to the fig tree, but also if ye shall say unto this mountain, Be thou removed, and be thou cast into the sea; it shall be done.'* If any doubt seeps into your faith in your return, it will not come."

A Tenfold Return is a demonstration within the consciousness of practically everyone. For example, most people can conceive of having ten times as much money as they now have in their pocket. Most people also have difficulty in conceiving of a greater multiplication, **at one time.** There is where doubt arises. One can reach the same goal progressively—without the strain which causes doubt.

Surely it is possible to demonstrate a larger than tenfold return. But keep in mind that even Jesus, the Christ Spirit personified, did not walk on water all of the time.

The young man learned the hidden wisdom in moderation.

* Matthew 21:21

A young lady had a more basic problem—one which prevented her tenfold return before she had even planted her Seed Money. She lacked gratitude; she never gave thanks for anything.

As John Hoshor writes: "The full figure of your return, however, is and **must be**, important to you—important enough to call forth from you **a fullhearted thankfulness** as well as the necessary mental work. **Gratitude is the open door to Abundance.** It helps to shorten the time required for your demonstration. Chemists tell us that for each ten degrees' increase in temperature the speed of a chemical reaction doubles. So add the warmth of thankfulness, of gratitude, to your Seed Money formula—all along the line."

Gratitude is an indispensable catalyst in the working of the Law of Tenfold Return.

I asked the young lady if she knew of the custom of saying Grace before meals.

She replied that she did.

"In saying Grace," I told her, "you are giving thanks to God before the object of the thanks has been received—**and as if it had already been received.**"

The sowing of Seed Money and the reaping of its harvest of multiplied return is exactly the same. Before we can expect more we must give thanks for that which we already have.

Everything is in its Source from God—what

we have received and what we are receiving through the Law of Tenfold Return, for "of him, and through him, and to him, are **all things.**"[*]

By giving thanks for what we already have —including that part which we are giving as Seed Money—we help to expand our Seed Money to its tenfold return.

Dr. Ervin Seale of the Church of the Truth, New York, says: "Expansion is the law of life." And Gratitude is an absolutely necessary part of expressing life.

Gratitude also serves as a magnet to attract our tenfold return to us.

When the young lady learned this—and consciously expressed gratitude in her life—she began to work the Law of Tenfold Return.

So many people—not yet understanding that as God is Substance, so is God the Source of the Tenfold Return—have omitted God in their attempts to practice Seed Money. They have not been keeping their eye upon the doughnut, but upon the hole.

God is Infinite **everything,** not limited **nothingness.**

This truth has seemed to create a paradox for some people who have rationalized that a specific Tenfold Return is a limitation.

This is not the case. As SEED MONEY

[*] Romans 11:36

says: "You may be told by someone that laying claim to a **specific** amount limits you. This is not the law. Claiming a specific amount makes the demonstration both easier and more rapid. Actually, you do not limit yourself by making a claim for a specific amount because you can apply and re-apply the principle an endless number of times either in succession or concurrently."

A practitioner worked the Principle of Seed Money and invariably received her Tenfold Return on Seed Money she had sown both in succession and concurrently. She could conceive of each gift's tenfold return without interference with the return on the other gifts. Most people, however, find it easier to practice the Law of Tenfold Return in succession.

Because of subtle negative thoughts which seem to originate with many people when they have "many irons in the fire," it is recommended that they, at first, sow their Seed Money in succession. Then each tenfold return helps to fortify faith in the next.

One of the doubts which may arrive especially in concurrent Seed Money harvesting is that regarding Source. This doubt also arises in single Seed Money demonstrations when the individual does not have firmly fixed in his consciousness that God is the Source of his Supply and that the words of Jesus, "Father, I thank thee that thou has heard me. And I knew that thou hearest me always,"* are as equally true today as they were in Palestine nearly two thousand years ago.

John Hoshor said: "Do not pay the slightest attention to WHERE your return is coming from. That is neither your work nor your responsibility. The Infinite—God—takes care of both the means and the manner. Your work is to claim the tenfold return of your gift and to leave all constructive ways open for it to reach you.

"Seed Money return is EXPECTED money return. The means by which it comes to you and the manner in which it comes to you may be unexpected—more than likely it will be unexpected—but the return itself is EXPECTED."

Because the way and manner of your tenfold return is generally unexpected, some people do not recognize their tenfold return, even when they have received it.

A part-time typist worked one day a week for a leading metropolitan newspaper. Her workday at the paper was Friday. One Friday she received from a friend a copy of SEED MONEY. That Sunday she made a special Seed Money donation to her Church.

* John 11:41/42

On the next Thursday she told the man in the newspaper office who had given her the booklet:

"Seed Money doesn't work. I still haven't received my return—although I believed 100%."

He questioned her: "But why are you working today—and also yesterday—when your only work-day here is on Fridays?"

"Oh," she replied, "I'm replacing a regular typist who went away on a short trip."

"Let me call the personnel office and see why you were picked for the extra work," the man who had given her the SEED MONEY booklet said.

Five minutes later he told the temporary typist:

"Personnel said there was no special reason for giving you the extra assignment—when the girl opened the page to the list of their qualified part-time typists her finger just fell by your name."

The typist's face suddenly glowed: "Oh, I did get my Tenfold Return after all. It is returned to me through the two unexpected extra days of work here — doing what I most enjoy doing."

She had received her tenfold return before she had given up. Some people always give up before they get their return because they set a

time limitation when they plant their Seed
Money. That is a great mistake.

A long time ago a Latin American public
official kept me waiting for several hours after
the appointment was due. When he finally arrived I said rather crossly: "Aren't any of you
Latin Americans ever on time?"

He replied, smilingly, "No, but we don't have
ulcers."

Ulcers, as medical science shows, are caused
by worry, and time limitations—which we our-
selves set and give power to—create most wor-
ries. Worry about man's measurement called time
can be halted by a realization that God knows
but one unit of time—NOW. It is said that
"tomorrow never comes." This is perfectly true,
for when tomorrow is here it is no longer tomorrow—but TODAY.

A woman who owned a gift shop repeatedly
planted Seed Money and repeatedly failed to
receive her tenfold return. She couldn't understand it, for she said: "I know that the Principle
of Seed Money works. Why doesn't it work for
me?"

We analyzed her problem. She always said:
I have received X dollars (tenfold the exact
sum given) in return, with good to all concerned. Thank you. Thank you. Thank you."

After talking it out, we found that she

always subconsciously added a future date for her return—whether for one day or one week later—which negated her statement that she had received the return.

I told her that we find the Promise in the Book of the Prophet Isaiah: "And it shall come to pass, that before they call, I will answer; and while they are yet speaking, I will hear."[*]

When we give our Seed Money and claim our return we must KNOW that our tenfold return has ALREADY been made. Any thought that the return will only be made in the future will postpone our return indefinitely.

The gift shop owner saw her error—dissolved all thoughts of time limitation—and thanked God for her return NOW, and she began working the Principle of Seed Money successfully.

SEED MONEY answers the question, "How long will it take?—

"There is no time in the Infinite. Time is a human concept. Do your work faithfully and go happily about your normal business. As certainly as the day will dawn on the morrow your effort will be rewarded."

John Hoshor also gave some helpful steps in practicing the Law of Tenfold Return:

"One of the best ways to attain proficiency in the operation of the Law is to repeat the Daily Affirmation, which closes this booklet, many

[*] Isaiah 65:24

times a day for many days until you have thoroughly convinced yourself WHO YOU ARE and WHAT YOUR PROPER ROLE IN THE UNIVERSE IS. Do this and the Law will work for you promptly and in full measure.

"There is also an after-the-fact technique which invariably helps to shorten the time required for demonstrations. It aids in registering the pattern clearly in your consciousness.

"Imagine that you have the return in hand. That much you MUST do. Then, to that add the mental picture of exactly what you are going to do with the money. If you intend to spend it, see yourself buying, choosing, exactly what you want. Also see yourself as wearing, or carrying, it out of the store after you have seen yourself paying for it. Go through the details of the transaction several times. What you said, what the sales person said, the store or stores in which you are going to make the purchase or purchases, put in all of the details.

"Or it may be that you are going to put the Seed Money return in your bank. Then see yourself going into the bank, making out the deposit slip, carrying it and the money over to the teller's window and speaking to the teller, giving him the money and the deposit slip and getting your receipt back. Imagine what the teller says to you and hear him saying it.

"Also imagine yourself sending another check

to your Church or to your favorite Social Service organization as the next step in utilizing this Unlimited and ever new Source of Wealth."

I know a businessman who could not practice the Law of Tenfold Return because of his mental attitude of lack. I explained to him:

"A good gardener does not only cultivate flowers—he cultivates SOIL. The thoughts which you are always sending out compose the soil of your life. If you are constantly projecting thoughts of lack you will have barren soil. If you project thoughts of prosperity your soil will be rich in the humus of success, and it is that soil in which your Seed Money grows.

Jesus tells us that in the parable of the sower:

"Behold, a sower went forth to sow:

"And when he sowed, some seeds fell by the way side, and the fowls came and devoured them up:

"Some fell upon stony places, where they had not much earth: and forthwith they sprung up, because they had no deepness of earth:

"And when the sun was up, they were scorched; and because they had no root, they withered away.

"And some fell among thorns; and the thorns sprung up, and choked them:

"But other fell into good ground, and brought forth fruit, some an hundredfold, some sixtyfold, some thirtyfold."*

* Matthew 13:3/8

The businessman said, "True, but how can I prepare my soil?"

I referred him to Dr. Raymond Charles Barker's wonderful booklet, MONEY IS GOD IN ACTION, and I advised him to treat for a prosperity consciousness.

Dr. Barker says: "All spiritual treatment is an action of the conscious on the subconscious. Treat this way, 'Money is God's Idea of circulation. This Idea, I accept. This Idea, I now accept. This Idea, I now accept as the basis of all my financial affairs. I like money. I believe that it is God's Activity, that it is good. I use it with wisdom. I release it with joy. I send it forth without fear, for I know that under a Divine Law, it comes back to me increased and multiplied.' If you will use this treatment, and subjectively accept it, you will be amazed at the results."

The businessman repeatedly made this treatment, and soon was able to reap abundant harvests from his Seed Money.

It is very important for us to get out of our mental patterns of poverty—to realize that, as God knows no lack, neither do we.

John Hoshor writes:

"The Law is there for you to use just as the fresh, wonderful air in the earth's atmosphere is there for you to breathe. Would you choose to spend your Life without fresh air? In a smoke-filled room or in an area constantly saturated

with smog? Such conditions take their toll in
Life and health for those who choose them or
permit themselves to live in such surroundings.
Similarly, those who are ignorant of the Law
of Seed Money, and of how it works, suffer with
unfulfilled needs, suffer from the lack of many
of the desirable things of Life which in our day
require money to buy.

"Human needs are greater today than they
have ever been.

"The cost of living, at or near a record high,
continues to mount. Rents are the highest ever
and are still increasing. Food and clothing were
never costlier. Today, all children—to be able
to compete with their own generation—must
have a college education.

"Wage and salary increases do not solve the
problem. Other and greater sources of money
income are needed.

"The saying that the rich get richer was
never truer. Or that the poor get poorer. The
reasons for both are fundamental. Most of the
rich are daily applying the Law, although they
may not be aware of it. They have a surplus
above their living needs which makes it unnecessary to pay any more than casual attention to
those needs. So they do not multiply NEEDS
in their consciousness. They live, surrounded by
riches and the evidences of riches, and with

riches filling their consciousness they continually attract more and greater riches to themselves.

"The Law always works. The direction in which it works depends solely upon the contents of the individual's consciousness.

"The poor are constantly thinking about what they NEED and forever talking about it. The Universal Law of Life is **that upon which you focus your attention always comes into your Life and experience.**

"The individual's only salvation is to get himself out of the vicious circle of need and poverty, to stop focusing on them and instead **focus on receiving, having, sharing and giving.**"

One woman said, "I can never even start to practice Seed Money because I can't even plant some Seed Money—I never have enough money to spare. I'm too poor."

I advised her to open her Bible to Proverbs, find Chapter 11, and then read Verse 24.

She read: "There is that scattereth, and yet increaseth; and there is that withholdeth more than is meet, but it tendeth to poverty."*

In other words, there are those who circulate that which they have, and what they have increases; and there are those who hold fast to every penny they have, and they become poverty stricken.

* Proverbs 11:24

This Verse from the Scriptures changed her way of thinking. It made her realize WHY she had been unable to increase what she had. She has become an ardent follower of the Law of Tenfold Return.

John Hoshor gave another example of how he helped someone to success through the Principle of Seed Money:

"A man I know by the name of Sheldon found a way out.

"This man had many ups and downs. He was twice a **millionaire,** both times when a million dollars was a lot of money. Some months ago Sheldon's business failed. The immediate cause was a bad credit loss. Yet he knew there was a deeper cause.

"I suggested to Sheldon the John D. Rockefeller technique of giving. When he answered that he had given not thousands, but hundreds of thousands, of dollars away I knew that he spoke the truth. Sheldon has never been known to refuse a request for help. I explained to him that although giving was necessary, **just giving was not enough,** that one can easily go bankrupt giving without return.

"He listened for an hour as I outlined the principle of Seed Money to him.

"Sheldon asked, 'With what do I start? I'm flat broke.'

"Actually he had $3 in his pocket. On my

advice he exchanged his $3 for 300 new pennies and started giving them out one at a time. I received the first one. Each time he gave a penny he would multiply it in his consciousness and see the multiplied return as having been made to him. The same evening, before he had given out all of his pennies, a long forgotten creditor came to his home and paid him $12 on an old bill.

"On my advice Sheldon went again to the bank and this time brought back 200 new nickels. Again he started giving them away, one at a time, each time following the Seed Money technique. Within three days he was called in as consultant on a marketing problem and received $250 for a half day's work.

"Still working the Seed Money formula this time he started with $100 worth of new quarters. While he was busy giving these out and multiplying and claiming his return two friends contacted him and offered to finance him in a new business venture. All the capital he needed was placed at his disposal.

"Sheldon came to my apartment and we talked over the situation.

"He said, 'Although I have been in business in New York City for 40 years, actually, like Moses, I have been wandering in the wilderness. Never before have I known what I was doing.' He insisted that he would not have any more 'downs' in his Life because he had learned the Seed Money formula and practiced it. He still gives but now he multiplies and claims his ten-fold return and his new business is prospering mightily."

We have seen that just giving is not enough to work the Law of Tenfold Return, but "WHY IS GIVING NECESSARY?"

John Hoshor says, "The farmer who wants a crop must give to the earth—must sow or plant the seed—otherwise he will harvest only weeds.

"When you were born the first thing the doctor did was to hold you up by the heels and smack your little bottom. You gave out with a squawk and that started you breathing. Breathing itself is both a giving and a receiving. So is your very Life, for discontinue either exhaling or inhaling and you cannot live.

"When you want the lights on you turn the switch which opens the circuit and starts the flow of current. The entire Universe is a series of energy circuits—from the earth and other planets in their orbits to the particles of the atom in their orbits. Shut off the flow anywhere along the line and the result is nothingness.

"In James Stephens' classic, "THE CROCK OF GOLD, the Old Philosopher observed, 'You must be fit to give before you can be fit to receive.'

"The plain and simple truth is that you must start giving before you can start receiving. This is the kind of Universe in which we live."

A secretary couldn't understand why prayer alone, without giving Seed Money, wouldn't work.

I told her that Prayer with Thanksgiving are complementary essentials, for "in every thing by prayer and supplication with thanksgiving let your request be made known unto God."[*] The gift itself not only subconsciously sets in motion a cycle of ever-increasing energy—which returns to you in your tenfold return—but it also serves to fix firmly in your mind the image of the desired return.

The story of the great prophet Elijah and the widow of Zarephath, where the widow's scant food supply multiplied so that she and the Prophet Elijah, "and her house, did eat many days,"[**] proves this Truth.

As Dr. Henry M. Ellis writes in his monumental book, BIBLE SCIENCE: THE TRUTH AND THE WAY:

"As Elijah proved, **an act of faith, evidenced by giving,** is prerequisite to receiving."

The importance of the **doing**—of actually giving—is shown not only in the Old and New

[*] Philippians 4:6
[**] I Kings 17:10/16

Testaments, but in other religious works through the ages. In the Koran, the Holy Book of the Moslems, we find:

"He that doeth good Shall have ten times As much to his credit."[*]

Omitting the actual sowing of Seed Money in the Law of Tenfold Return is the same as sewing without thread—you make a lot of motion, but you don't get anywhere.

The secretary accepted this, and with some further help, was able to practice the Law of Tenfold Return. She was more fortunate than a man who, receiving a SEED MONEY booklet, complained that he had not a penny to his name —he had spent his last fifteen cents on a bowl of soup.

I turned his booklet to the page in SEED MONEY which states:

"How can I give when I don't have any money?

"Then you must start with your muscles, with labor and the sweat of thy brow until you have received some of the currency of the realm. Then start giving it and claiming the multiplication of the tenfold return back to yourself. Continue this as you continue breathing and soon you will be prosperous and surrounded by Abundance.

"Actually, no one ever grew rich working

[*]Sura VI:160

either at labor or at a white collar job. Those who grow rich are those who organize their minds for riches, who direct employees on the one hand and who direct their multiplied claims to the Infinite on the other hand. As a matter of fact, you do not need any employees to become rich, provided you know the Seed Money technique and use it persistently. Likewise, you can be an employee and by using the Seed Money formula constantly in your Life you can become wealthier than your employer, if he fails to use the formula."

The "down-and-out" man said, "Who would hire me?"

I said, "We have some packages to take to the Post Office right now—you can Seed Money your labor and I will give you a dollar besides."

He said, "What? Manual labor? Never." He ran from the office, leaving his SEED MONEY booklet behind. I tried to catch him, but he had gotten into the elevator before I was able to do so.

This man had counted himself "down-and-out." He will not get up off of the canvas until he realizes that the Law of Tenfold Return decrees that ten times something is that something multiplied by ten. Ten times nothing, however, is always nothing.

An engineer understood this perfectly. He saw that the Law of Tenfold Return was based upon a perfectly logical working of the Power of the Mind—a Part of the Universal One Mind.

But, every time he planted Seed Money he began to wonder and speculate as to HOW and by what mechanics his return would come. He was not getting his tenfold return.

His problem was very simple. He did not exercise unquestioning faith. He did not "let go, and let God."

SEED MONEY states: "Do you remember the saying, 'A little child shall lead them?' Why shall a little child lead them? Because it is easy for a child to imagine, and because children practice imagining more than grownups do."

Jesus said, "Yea; have ye never read, Out of the mouth of babes and sucklings thou hast perfected praise?"[*]

The engineer was advised to **claim** his expected return **now**, and leave the working of his tenfold return to God, and he saw that as a child can unquestioningly accept that good inevitably produces good, so can he unquestioningly see the multiplication of his Seed Money. After all, Jesus had expressed this Truth, "For a good tree bringeth not forth corrupt fruit; neither doth a corrupt tree bring forth good fruit. For every tree is known by its own fruit. For of thorns men do not gather figs, nor of a bramble bush gather they grapes."[**]

[*] Matthew 21:16
[**] Luke 6:43/44

Recognizing that the Law of Tenfold Return is part of the Universal One Law, the engineer applied to his practice of the Seed Money Principle the same childlike faith required in All Spiritual Unfoldment, as Jesus said, "Whosoever shall not receive the kingdom of God as a little child, he shall not enter therein."*

The engineer's new success in demonstrating through the Law of Tenfold Return was based upon his understanding that it is a formula originating through Jesus.

As John Hoshor wrote in SEED MONEY:

"What is the formula which makes the Law of Seed Money work for you?

"**The formula is derived from Jesus. When properly used, it always produces the desired results.**"

Jesus declared very clearly:

"**What things soever ye desire, when ye pray, believe that ye receive them, and ye shall have them.**"**

AND THAT IS EXACTLY WHAT HE MEANT.

Quoting from SEED MONEY, "No words ever spoken or written in any language carry greater, or more far-reaching, import than these words of the Great Master.

"Please note:

"You are not asked to join any organization.

*Mark 10:15
**Mark 11:24

"You are not asked to attend any meetings.

"You are not asked to subscribe to any dogma.

"You are not asked to follow any ritual.

"You are not asked to believe any theories, opinions or suppositions.

"You are only asked to believe that you already have received whatever it is you want.

"Surely this is not too great a price for you to pay to achieve your desires.

"Imagine that they are yours NOW.

"What could be easier?

"And it works. It works. IT WORKS. Anyone can prove it conclusively for himself.

"To repeat, the ONLY THING which you have to believe is that you have already received that which you want. Your age does not matter. Your creed does not matter. Your race does not matter. Your name does not matter. Your sex does not matter. Your political affiliations do not matter. Your nationality does not matter. Your education does not matter.

"Simply believe that YOU HAVE ALREADY RECEIVED WHATEVER IT IS YOU WANT. No one else can limit you. If you want to limit yourself, you can. Otherwise the entire resources of the Universe may be yours to use."

One lady who had come to the United States from Eastern Europe wasn't having success with her practice of the Seed Money formula. She had a subconscious pattern of limitation, due to an image of herself in her own mind that she, as a refugee, was a second-class citizen. She compounded the damage to herself by constantly dwelling on what she had lost instead of on the HERE and NOW. She resented everyone who owned fine things such as she had lost.

With help, in time she realized that God knows only one class—FIRST—and that she, as a child of God, was the sole person who could possibly even seem to demote her in Reality.

She saw that she, not only in order to bring prosperity through the Law of Tenfold Return into her life, but in order to attain peace of mind, had to obey the commandments as Jesus had stated them:

"And thou shalt love the Lord thy God with all they heart, and with all they soul, and with all thy mind, and with all thy strength: this is the first commandment.

"And the second is like, namely this, Thou shalt love they neighbour as theyself. There is none other commandment greater than these."°

Only then did she realize that she must lose her resentments against her neighbors.

Through persistent meditation on these two greatest commandments and their place in her

° Mark 12:30/31

Life she suddenly found herself able to make the demonstrations which she, and she alone, had blocked for so long.

She turned her once-lonely life of self-punishment into a happy Life of Abundance and helpfulness to others.

This helpfulness—a willingness and readiness to lend a helpful hand—often provides opportunities to sow Seed Money under circumstances in which it is remarkably easy to visualize a return—Good for Good, multiplied tenfold.

John Hoshor related in SEED MONEY:

"One morning not long ago I was waiting on a street corner in Manhattan for a bus to take me to my office. A man who had been sitting on a nearby bench arose and shuffled over to where I stood.

"We spoke and passed the time of day. I noticed that his clothes were old and torn and that instead of shoes he was wearing low-cut rubber overshoes. I asked the question which he had obviously expected me to ask.

" 'What happened to your shoes?'

" 'Someone stole them while I was asleep last night,' he told me.

" 'What are you going to do for shoes?'

" 'That is what I have been wondering. I found these in the garbage back of the building where I slept,' he answered. He showed me the soles which were more holes than rubber.

" 'What can you get a pair of shoes for?' I asked.

" 'There's a Shoe Repair place I know where I can get an unclaimed repaired pair for $4 or maybe $5.'

"Then I asked him, 'Do you have the money?'

" 'I don't have a cent,' he replied.

" 'How near is the Shoe Repair place?' I asked.

"He pointed, 'Only two blocks over that way.'

" 'Let's walk over,' I suggested.

"When we reached the Repair Store I handed him $5.

" 'See what you can get with that. If you need more, tap on the window and I will come in.'

"In a few minutes he came out of the store wearing a comfortable looking pair of repaired shoes. He held out a dollar bill towards me, saying, 'I got these for 4 bucks.'

" 'Keep the dollar,' I told him.

"We walked together to the corner and shook hands, thanking each other.

"He asked, 'Why do you thank me?'

" 'Because I am happy that I was able to be of service to you,' I told him.

"We wished each other good luck and I went on my way to the bus stop.

"As I walked I silently repeated over and over again the Seed Money formula. 'I have received $50 in return. I have received $50 in return with good to all concerned. Thank you.

Thank you. Thank you.' When I arrived at my office business took over and I forgot the incident.

"Mind you, please, I have practiced the formula for hours and hours over the years. I have worked it almost countless times, both on a small scale and on a large scale. I have seen friends make it work many times. So not only did I believe I had received the $50 in return, I knew. I knew. I KNEW.

"That night as I opened the door of the apartment house in which I live a pretty girl came out and smilingly thanked me. I noticed she carried a musical score from 'The Pajama Game' and asked her,

" 'Are you a singer?'

" 'No,' she answered, 'I'm a receptionist, but I'm taking singing lessons.'

' "Who is your teacher?' I asked.

"She mentioned the name of a voice teacher who had been a friend of mine for many years but whom I had not seen for 15 years. I told her my name and asked her to remember me to her teacher. She said that she would and went on her way.

"I went to my apartment, showered and put on fresh clothes. As I was starting out to keep an appointment, the manager of the apartment house came to my door and told me I had a call over her phone. I answered it. The voice teacher was calling and asked me to come to his studio. I went at 10:30 that evening. After we had shaken hands and congratulated each other on none of the 15 years showing, he said,

" 'John, before you moved to California, you did some publicity for me which proved very profitable to me. You never sent me a bill.'

"I explained that I had done it as a favor, that it had not required any time, merely a phone call.

"He said, 'Had you billed me then, I could not have paid you, but I would like to pay you now.'

"He walked over to the Baby Grand piano and picked up a check already made out and offered it to me, saying,

" 'Will $50 be all right?'

"I answered him, '$50 is exactly right.'

"There may be some who will scoff and say that I have linked two events which had no fundamental relationship to each other. However, the wiser will believe me when I say that the $5 given to the needy man for the shoes and the $50 out of the blue for a forgotten service were as certainly linked to each other as my fingers are linked to my hands.

"Here was a penniless, needy man, in rags, without shoes, who unknowingly brought to me $45 in profit, in added Wealth and Prosperity, which it is conceivable, might never have otherwise reached me. How was this possible? It was possible only because I knew the Principle of Seed Money, the Law of Tenfold Return, and I took the opportunity which came my way to aid a fellow human being and of then applying the Law and claiming my multiplied return. I thanked him sincerely before we parted and should he ever read this, I thank him again."

A unique way of sowing Seed Money was that of the Advertising Manager of a magazine. He read a copy of SEED MONEY and said that he wanted to Seed Money space in his magazine to advertise the booklet.

He did. For nearly a year his advertising revenue increased substantially, which he credits to his practice of Seed Money.

The practice of Seed Money, from generation to generation, can produce wealth which is hardly conceivable to the average man. When he sees a work of art, hears beautiful music, receives the most modern medical treatment, or sees our rockets soaring into space, he may not know that many of the achievements in these fields would not have been possible without the practice of Seed Money by the Guggenheim family.

From 1847, when Meyer Guggenheim immigrated to America, until today, a fortune which has conservatively been estimated at $200,-000,000 has circulated and increased for but one purpose, as Amabassador Harry Guggenheim says, "for the progress of man."

The benefits the great Guggenheim wealth have given mankind—through financing, building and developing—are inestimable, and the selection of the title of the Guggenheim family biography bears witness to its growth: SEED MONEY.

The thinking of the Guggenheim family has been the very opposite of lack. The word "can't" doesn't seem to be in their vocabulary. And the ability to know that success is here, **even before it has been visibly manifested,** has not only characterized the Guggenheim success, but is an indispensable factor in practicing Seed Money.

As John Hoshor says: "So that there can be no vagueness or misunderstanding in the mind of any reader as to how he makes his claim on the Infinite for the multiplied return of his gift, I wish to point out that he does so by **believing he has already received such multiplied return.** It is as simple as that.

"Instead of **continually saying, as many do, 'I want,' 'I need,' or 'I do not have,'** say, 'I have,' 'I have,' 'I have,' 'I HAVE.'

"In addition to making the gift to start the flow of prosperity to you, believing that you have ALREADY received your multiplied return IS YOUR ONLY WORK.

"Practice this art of believing specifically as an actor practices his lines, as a champion golfer practices his swing, as a great concert pianist practices on his instrument. There is no other endeavor in Life which will pay off so well. Begin the practice now, if you want to grow exceedingly prosperous and rise above all the want and lack, and have great riches in their place."

An Army sergeant was having trouble practicing the Seed Money Principle. It seemed that this man—who had, through prayer, recovered from a nearly fatal wound—could not exercise his faith on money matters.

I read to him from the Scriptures, "be ye transformed by the renewing of your mind, that ye may prove what is that good, and acceptable. and perfect, will of God."[*]

He practiced the Seed Money Principle anew, step by step. He had one small success, several failures. He did not give up.

He gave, not loaned, but gave as Seed Money, ten dollars to a private who was going home on emergency leave. Then the results started for the sergeant.

Shortly after the Korean War he had been in the hospital for six months. He had started to paint as physical therapy, had liked it, and had made painting his hobby. On the week-end

* Romans 12:2

after he had planted the ten dollars Seed Money a man happened to pass by while he was painting. He liked the sergeant's picture and bought it—for one hundred dollars.

The sergeant is now retired, augmenting his pension by selling his paintings. This unexpected source of income, and enjoyment, the sergeant credits to Seed Money.

Some, from complete adversity, work the Law of Tenfold Return on the very first attempt. John Hoshor gives an example:

"There was a woman neighbor of mine in Hollywood who was on the verge of committing suicide because she could not find work. She had borrowed all she could from friends and pawned everything pawnable.

"After hours of talking with her she agreed to give and did give $6.50 of her last $7.20 to The Salvation Army. Within three days she received a Cashier's Check from a son from whom she had not heard in five years. After buying food and paying a week's rent she had $20 left. She told me rather sheepishly that she had taken $15 of that and given it to The Salvation Army. She said,

" 'It worked once. I hope it will work again.'

"I explained to her that when you work with the Law, you do not heed to 'hope.' You know!"

Hope can be wishful thinking, and our thinking in the practice of the Law of Tenfold Return must not be "wishful" — but "knowing." Hoping to get your tenfold return implies a wavering, and this is very damaging, as is said in James: "But let him ask in faith, nothing wavering. For he that wavereth is like a wave of the sea driven with the wind and tossed."[*]

If you toss the ship bearing your tenfold return by wavering, by only hoping that it will reach its port, it never will.

John Hoshor recounts the story of a man who wavered both before he made his Seed Money planting and before he made his claim for his tenfold return. Once doing the steps, however, the man never wavered.

"This man, Carroll, now has a gift shop in Los Angeles. When he was struggling, trying to save enough money to open the shop he had a letter from a nine year old niece of whom he was very fond. The niece asked him to lend to her $300 so that she could have her teeth straightened. Carroll told me about the request. He showed me the little girl's picture, saying she was the prettiest child he had ever seen. The picture showed that she was pretty. But Carroll said,

" 'I can't lend her the money. I have less than $1,000 and I need more than $3,000 to open a Gift Shop. It will take her years and years to repay me.'

[*] James 1:6

"He continued talking about it. Finally he asked my advice.

" 'Don't lend her the money by any means,' I told him. **'Give it to her.** Send it to her today.

"After hours of discussion I convinced him that it was the right thing to do, not only for the sake of his niece, but even more, for his own sake.

"Carroll sent his niece the money. I think that for a while he was sorry because it took more hours of talk to get him to make his multiplied claim for his return. He agreed, however, and did make his claim.

"The following Sunday, Carroll telephoned me. He may not have had tears in his eyes, but he surely had them in his voice. A former partner from whom Carroll had been estranged for 12 years or more came to Carroll's home and handed him thirty new one hundred dollar bills. The ex-partner told Carroll that when they had dissolved the business years before, Carroll had been defrauded out of certain moneys. The $3,000 represented this money with interest. Carroll opened his gift shop the following month."

Another example of the working of the Seed Money Principle, this time where the man had no hesitations, is given by John Hoshor:

"A novelist friend of mine, working on a novel, wanted to go to the British West Indies for three months and finish his book there. He

gave me no argument but went to his bank as I
had told him to do, and drew out his last $70
and gave it to his Church. He also followed the
formula with enthusiasm. In less than a week
I saw him off to the British West Indies. A pub-
lisher whom he had not previously known had
contacted him and employed him to do a series
of three magazine articles on those islands. My
friend received a $500 advance **plus** a check of
$200 on account of his expenses."

In each case the recipient of Seed Money
always benefits—with no loss to anyone else. This
is ensured by the phrase, "with good to all concerned." **This phrase should always be included
when you make your claim for your tenfold
return.**

You are all probably familiar with the tale
of the man who was granted three wishes by a
witch. With the granting of each wish he
received his expressed desire accompanied by a
far greater loss. That story is a fable, of course,
but when exercising your mental powers within
the structure of anything as potent as the Law
of Tenfold Return you must carefully avoid
anything which might be MENTAL MAL-
PRACTICE.

We find in Genesis that "God saw every
thing that he had made, and, behold, it was
very good."° God is Good, All Good, and when

° Genesis 1.31

you declare that your tenfold return is "with good to all concerned" you are keeping the entire transaction on the proper mental plateau, "very good" in every respect.

As it says in SEED MONEY, "There is no telling how the return which you claim will come to you. The only telling for certain is that it will come. You do not want some loved one to die and will to you the amount you claim. You do not want to receive it as a result of an injury to yourself. So always, always, ALWAYS, include in your multiplied Seed Money claim, or for that matter whenever you draw upon the Infinite for anything, the provision "with good to all concerned." In this manner you protect yourself and others who may be concerned.

"Carefully check your motive in each of your Seed Money operations to make certain that there is no content of harm, or intended harm, in it towards anyone concerned. Whether the money is primarily for yourself, or for others, or simply for reserve to practice proving the Law, it should manifest with equal ease. The Law does not care. But if there is harm in your consciousness towards anyone, that harm will multiply also and return to fall upon your own head. You cannot fool, or sidestep, the Law."

This is equally true in regard to your physical health, as well as your financial health, for God is the Source of All Good and "no good thing will be withheld from them that walk uprightly."°

As John Hoshor explained: "In the times of the Great Teacher very little was known regarding human health. Disease was rampant. Almost everyone was ill. Life expectancy at birth was extremely low. Even in Shakespeare's day it was reported as having been 4 years.

"Much of the ministry of Jesus was devoted to healing those who had little or no other chance of health. Today we have a great medical science, mammoth and well-equipped, ably staffed hospitals in every area. We have physicians' offices in almost every block, with expensive research laboratories dotting our land.

"Dr. Arnold A. Hutschnecker, a physician who has practiced internal medicine in New York City for more than 40 years, states in his book, THE WILL TO LIVE, that in spite of a long succession of miracle drugs and great advances in medical knowledge, about one-half of the people in the world are ill at any given time.

"In contrast, 99% of all of the people in the world are living hand-to-mouth—in the face of the greatest prosperity the human race has ever witnessed. It is our opinion that were Jesus alive today he would devote some of his time and

° Psalms 84:11

teachings to telling his listeners how to become prosperous.

"Can't you just hear this Great Teacher saying, 'Your lack, your needs, your poverty, are insults to the Father. These are totally unnecessary conditions which you have pinned upon yourself. Rise above your ignorance. Find out WHO YOU ARE and make your claim for an Overflowing Abundance of all of the good things of Life, and it shall be given to you, in full and running over.'

"Then again, 'With what measure you give, it shall be multiplied tenfold and given back to you.' "

A girl in her twenties wished to practice the Seed Money Principle, but seemed unable to work the Law of Tenfold Return. When I saw her I noticed a very pronounced limp when she walked. She said that she wanted her Tenfold Return for the purpose of paying for extensive physical therapy sessions.

I asked her, "How did you limp come about?"

She replied, "I was in an automobile accident—the driver was drunk—and I was nearly killed."

I asked her if a nerve had been severed in her leg.

She said, "No, the doctor says there is nothing organically wrong—I only need to practice using my leg."

I told her, "Many times a person's physical and financial health are directly linked. I want you to try four simple steps."

She agreed to try, saying "I have nothing to lose."

First, she agreed to **FORGIVE** the man whose negligence had caused the accident in which she had been hurt.

Second, she agreed to **THANK GOD** for her breath of Life which might have been snuffed out in the accident.

Third, she agreed to **BELIEVE** that her leg was healed—accepting for herself the promise of Jesus, "As thou hast believed, so be it done unto thee."°

Fourth, she agreed to **KNOW** that as "thy faith hath made thee whole°° in the matter of her leg, so has her faith returned tenfold her Seed Money.

Through these four steps the girl found herself able to practice the Seed Money formula. She received enough money to enable her to pay for the physical therapy sessions; she then found her improvement so rapid that she soon discontinued them, pronounced "cured."

It may be said that she should have obtained a total healing of her leg before she was able to go on to the healing of her financial affairs.

° Matthew 8:13
°° Matthew 9:22

This is not necessarily so. God is not only Omniscient — ALL KNOWING — but Omniscience: ALL KNOWLEDGE. Medical knowledge is as much a part of God as is any other kind of knowledge. Through whichever channel God heals, as through whichever channel one receives his Tenfold Return, matters not one bit. What IS important is that "in due season we shall reap, if we faint not."[*]

In the practice of Seed Money, as in healing, it is not important HOW we reap—it is only important HOW we sow.

SEED MONEY states: "**The spirit in which you give is the most important thing about your gift.**

"Why?

"It is intrinsic to the pattern in your consciousness and its physical counterpart will carry through into your multiplied return.

"When an opportunity to give is offered to you, if you consider giving and then decide against it, saying in effect, 'I better not, I may need it myself,' **you will most certainly need it yourself.**

"If you give grudgingly or calculatingly these configurations will be present in your return.

"If, however, you give boldly, generously, full-heartedly, impulsively, it shall be given to you tenfold in the same manner."

[*]Galatians 6:9

This is explained very clearly in the Bible:

"He which soweth sparingly shall reap also sparingly; and he which soweth bountifully shall reap also bountifully.

"Every man according as he purposeth in his heart, so let him give; not grudgingly, or of necessity: for God loveth a cheerful giver."*

Never pass by an opportunity to sow Seed Money. A LOST OPPORTUNITY TO GIVE IS A LOST OPPORTUNITY TO RECEIVE.

John Hoshor illustrates this in an incident which happened to him:

"The fastest and in some ways most interesting return on a SEED MONEY tenfold claim that I know happened to me quite recently.

"I was on my way to a branch Post Office with an armload of parcel post. In addition, I carried—unwrapped, but in its own display package—a small appliance I was then distributing. I intended to deliver it to a local purchaser on my way back.

"As I hurried up the crowded street I passed a blind man with a cup. I thought to myself, 'I'd give him something if I weren't loaded down.'

"Almost instantly I recognized the negative application of the Law. I turned and struggled back through the crowd, reached the blind man and asked him to stop for a second.

* II Corinthians 9:6/7

"I laid my packages on the sidewalk, took all the change from my pocket and put it in his cup. It made a good noise and it seemed as if he were almost on the verge of opening his eyes. However, he did not, but repeated his thanks. I recovered my packages, reached the Post Office and mailed them. Then, taking my unwrapped appliance, I turned to leave the Post Office. A man stopped me, saying,

" 'I'm interested in that product. May I see it?'

" 'Certainly,' I answered.

"We stopped at the first writing counter near the entrance and I took the appliance out of its box and showed him how it worked. It happened to operate on batteries and their sound attracted a small crowd. The man who had inquired looked at it, then handed me his card, saying,

" 'Please mail us a catalog sheet. We may give you an order.'

"I thanked him and proceeded to put the product back in its box. Most of those who had been watching had disappeared. However, one man stepped up to me and said,

" 'Where can I buy a couple hundred of those things?'

" 'I distribute them,' I told him. 'I'll be happy to supply you.'

"He said, 'First, let me buy the Special Delivery stamp I came for, then we'll do some business.'

"On the way to my office he introduced himself. He was the Ohio distributor for one of the Reducing Foods and was in New York looking for a product he could use as a premium to open accounts with dealers. He bought 200, did not ask for the discount to which he was entitled and which I gave him. He paid cash. I do not know exactly how much I gave the blind man. I had made my claim for a general tenfold return, and I'm quite certain that the profit from that sale represented a full measure return, running over.

"Perhaps the most significant part of the transaction was that the buyer was as happy with his purchase as a child is with a shining new toy."

Here was John Hoshor himself receiving a tenfold return in accordance with the Law of Seed Money.

THE LAW OF SEED MONEY is in itself very simple:

"In giving money to your Church or school or college or hospital or to any Social Service organization or in any other way using money to bless, help or aid your fellow beings, you have not only the right and the privilege but you have also the duty of claiming from the Infinite a tenfold money return. To claim it is to receive it."

THE LAW OF SEED MONEY is the Key to using the Infinite Substance of God: "Now he that ministereth seed to the sower both minister bread for your food, and **multiply your seed sown, and increase the fruits of your righteousness.**"°

THE LAW OF SEED MONEY works in accordance with the WORDS of Jesus:

"All things, whatsoever ye shall ask in prayer, believing, ye shall receive."°°

THE FORMULA FOR PRACTICING SEED MONEY is only a way to help you to prove those words in your own experience.

THE FORMULA is very simple:

"1. Plant the SEED MONEY. Give the amount you wish to the organization or person you wish.

"2. Now you cultivate your claim. Immediately after you make your gift, and as soon as you are alone, make your tenfold claim on the Infinite in the following manner:

'I have received $ . . . (tenfold the exact sum given) in return, with good to all concerned. Thank you. Thank you. Thank you.'

"3. Repeat your formula, time and again.

° II Corinthians 9:10
°° Matthew 21:22

Say it just before you fall asleep. Say it during the night if you awaken. Say it several times the first thing in the morning. Do it enough and then relax and follow your normal routine. It is not necessary to overwork.

"4. Start your work at a modest level, high enough that your gift and your multiplied return are both important to you, so that you will do the work as outlined conscientiously. If you start at too high a level so that you may begin to wonder from where all the money is coming, you are liable to incur doubts. Avoid doubts or they will manifest in your results as nothingness.

"5. Tell no one of your claim or work. Do it in private. You may do it silently or aloud. You may also write your claim or claims and refer to them at times, to refresh your pattern. The only work you have to do is to impress the pattern on your own consciousness.

"6. In the event that your multiplied claim is not returned as rapidly as you think it should be after you have made your gift and done the work on your claim to the best of your ability, then do the following:

"Refer to the Daily Affirmation at the end of this book. Read it and re-read it until you know WHO YOU ARE. As soon as you realize WHO YOU ARE your demonstrations will fly on wings to you. People will shove money at you, if you claim money, from every side. You'll be literally able to pick it out of the air.

"7. Give your gift in the spirit of complete trust. Give it boldly, happily, impulsively, full-heartedly and generously. It will return to you tenfold in the physical counterpart of those qualities.

"Know that the Law is always in operation. The formula works in your favor when you work it. No one else can do it for you. You must do it for yourself just as you must breathe for yourself."

SEED MONEY explains why the Law of Seed Money and the Seed Money formula work, and why you must "believe you have already received" before you can receive:

"We are going to give you the reason it works and, should you ever fail to make it work, the reason why you fail. We are going to give you the only explanation which is the basis of all religions, all creeds, all faiths, all healings, all miracles and all of the conditions and experiences in human life.

"We are going to take the mystery out of all of these things and, in the golden words of the Rev. Paul M. Brunet, 'put the MASTERY in.'

"The ancient Hindu Emperor, Asoka, is reported to have observed, 'all creeds have their

miracles.' Today we not only know that this is
true, but we also know that the psychiatrists
and hypnotists have their miracles, too.

"Why?

"Because of man's relationship to the Universe.

"Scientists have explored the Universe with
powerful telescopes and with powerful micro-
scopes. In all of their search and research they
have found only one thing. From the farthest
star to the most infinitestimal part of the atom
the only thing scientists have been able to find
is **energy.**

"Energy fills the Universe.

"The Universe is Energy.

"The Infinite is ENERGY.

"Then it should surprise no one to learn that
there is a fluid, plastic, invisible Energy which
flows evermore through the human mind.

"This E n e r g y, Undifferentiated, flows
through the mind of **every** human being.

"This Infinite Energy which flows through
the human mind is Power, Sheer Power. It
enters your mind unformed and flows out of
your mind impressed with the pattern in your
consciousness and flows evermore into the
EXACT form of those patterns.

"This Infinite Energy which flows through
your mind is blind, has no will of its own, cannot

say no to your patterns or do anything but follow them explicitly.

"This Infinite Energy which evermore flows through your mind is Unlimited. It will flow into whatever pattern you conceive and inasmuch as all Energy works in a circuit, the Energy which flows through your mind brings back to you of its invisible circuit the physical counterpart of your thoughts, words and emotions.

"If you pattern the Infinite Energy which flows through your mind with a lack of good, a lack of good will appear to be returned to you.

"If you pattern it with disease, DIS-EASE will be returned to you.

"If you pattern this Energy with debts and needs, debts and needs will seem to be returned to you.

"If you pattern this Unlimited Infinite Energy which flows through your mind with Happiness, Happiness will be returned to you.

"If you pattern this Energy with great riches, great riches will be returned to you.

"If you pattern this Energy with Perfect Health, Perfect Health will be returned to you.

"If you pattern this Energy with Ever-renewing Life, with inexhaustible Vitality, with Everlasting Youth and with an Overflowing Abundance of all of the other good things of

Life, all of these wonderful things will be returned to you.

"You are the Director, the Selector, the Chooser, the Decider—you are the Absolute Monarch of that Infinite, Unlimited, Obeying, All-Powerful Energy which flows through your mind.

"Do you think that Nuclear Power is great? You're right. It is great, very great. But compared to the Infinite Energy which flows constantly through your mind, and of which YOU are the Undisputed Ruler, Nuclear Power is a weak and helpless infant in the arms of a mighty giant.

"The purpose of your Life, the responsibility of your Being, is to direct that Energy into the best and most constructive forms of which you can conceive. As you do so, you prosper. As you fail in this purpose—in this responsibility—you suffer."

Infinite Energy is the Power provided by God for man to use to realize his likeness to Him, for "God created man in his own image, in the image of God created he him."•

Infinite Energy is the Means for man to make his thoughts come to pass, for "Thou shalt also decree a thing, and it shall be established unto thee."••

• Genesis 1:27
•• Job 22:28

As is written in SEED MONEY:

"Now do you KNOW WHO YOU ARE?

"Now do you KNOW why you can make your SEED MONEY tenfold claims on the Infinite and have them paid in full?

"Infinite Energy is your Servant. It works every second of your Life FOR YOU, follows your EVERY order, has nothing else in all the world to do but to bring you Blessings, Health, Ever-renewing Life, Wealth, Prosperity and an Overflowing Abundance of all the good things of Life including deep and satisfying Happiness.

"Getting, having, enjoying and sharing all of these things are both your birthright and your duty."

And the Seed Money Principle, The Law of Tenfold Return, is a way to obtain these "loaves and fishes." These are necessary material things of Life—"for your heavenly Father knoweth that ye have need of all these things"—but never lose sight of the fact that they are only a part of an Unfolding, Rising Consciousness:

"But seek ye first the kingdom of God, and his righteousness: and all these things shall be added unto you."*

AND, "the kingdom of God is within you."**
THE PRINCIPLE OF SEED MONEY SHALL HELP YOU FIND IT.

* Matthew 6:32/33
** Luke 17:20

MY DAILY AFFIRMATION

I know WHO I AM.

I AM the Selector, the Director, the Guide, the Pattern Maker, the Blueprinter of that Unlimited, Unformed yet All-Powerful, Completely Obeying, Infinite Energy which every instant of my Life flows through my mind.

I AM the Eyes, the fingertips, the Consciousness of that Infinite Energy.

I AM the Sole Ruler and Absolute Monarch of that Infinite Energy which flows through my mind.

That Infinite Energy is my Omnipotent and Willing Servant, follows exactly my every order.

My words and thoughts and emotions FORM that Infinite Energy into the conditions and circumstances of my Life and environment. That All-Powerful Infinite Energy is constantly and precisely fulfilling—transforming—my words and thoughts and emotions into their physical counterparts.

No words or thoughts or emotions of mine ever return to me unfilled. Therefore, I am always exceedingly careful that all my words and thoughts and emotions are beneficial, positive, constructive and specific in all of their aspects.

By Guiding and Directing that Infinite Energy forever flowing throu;h my mind with words and thoughts and emotions which ARE beneficial, positive, constructive and specific, I bless myself with Perfect Health, with Ever-renewing Life, with Inexhaustible Vitality, with Everlasting Youthfulness, with Wisdom and Understanding, with Wealth, Prosperity, Happiness and an Overflowing Abundance of All Good things of Life.

I bless my fellow beings with beneficial, positive, constructive and specific words and thoughts and emotions and also with gifts of money, services, aid, help, love, praise and encouragement and claim my tenfold return on all of these from the Infinite as is both my privilege and my duty as a Conscious Expression of the Source of that Infinite Energy.

That Always Obedient, All-Powerful Infinite Energy which flows constantly through my mind ALWAYS brings my tenfold return to me. Daily my capacity to receive increases, expands and magnifies.

All Good completely fills my Life and environment and the Lives and environments of all of my fellow beings.

All Good is formed from All-Powerful, All-

Present, All-Knowing Infinite Energy which is MINE TO USE HERE AND NOW and is from God, All-Power, All-Presence, All-Knowledge.

And I AM One with God.

So I AM.

So is it.

SEED MONEY RECORD

Date...............Amount of Gift $.......... to...............
Return data ....
Date...............Amount of Gift $.......... to...............
Return data ....
Date...............Amount of Gift $.......... to...............
Return data ....
Date...............Amount of Gift $.......... to...............
Return data ....
Date...............Amount of Gift $.......... to...............
Return data ....
Date...............Amount of Gift $.......... to...............
Return data ....
Date...............Amount of Gift $.......... to...............
Return data ....
Date...............Amount of Gift $.......... to...............
Return data ....
Date...............Amount of Gift $.......... to...............
Return data ....
Date...............Amount of Gift $.......... to...............
Return data ....
Date...............Amount of Gift $.......... to...............
Return data ....